Some friends to Clay Pond even arrived in pairs.

Freddie and Thad were friends from another pond and decided to check out Clay Pond.

This would be the new home for both the frog and the toad!

CLAY POND
Freddie The Frog & Thaddeus Toad
Don G. Ford

Cover artwork and Story: Don Ford
Publisher's Note:

Dedication

This Book is dedicated to readers who enjoy good storytelling; in fiction. The kids will certainly smile when reading it, or having it read to them.

CLAY POND

Freddie the Frog

and Thaddeus Toad

The other day I took a little walk down to Clay Pond to see what was happening. Every day was different from the day before. New friends arrived on a regular basis to check out stories that have developed here over the years. Some are looking for new friends; others a possible new place to live. Many are just visiting, since they are so curious.

Sometimes duck hunters hide in the tall grasses around the pond. On occasion they reduce the population by a duck or two when they arrive. The residents are always thrilled when these men finally leave the pond. The pond will always have its scary times and its ups and downs.

Clay Pond has a rich history that is shared by other residents of the pond. Ask anyone there about the friendly turtle, and the other wonderful friends

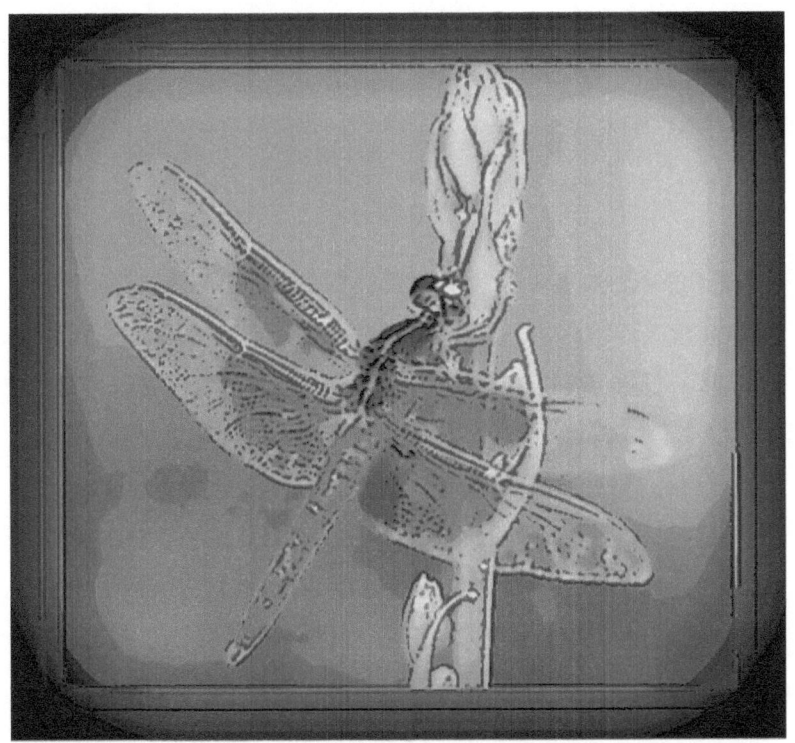

like Lacy the Dragonfly, who have made this place a home over the past several years.

Each creature has their own unique tale to tell. Everyone in this place looks out for the well being of all the others. If it were possible to claim each other as family, they would do it in a heartbeat. It is, in a word, a **safe haven** for anyone living in or around the pond.

Dear Newbie frog,

There are a few things that I must share with you about your new world. It will be quite different from the one you knew in that lower realm. Things on the surface are a whole lot different. The food you will eat now will be worlds apart from your earlier menu. Even you are different in this changing world you now are seeing.

You are bigger and your appetite has grown. It is a new food you will be eating, nothing like the old stuff you were used to. This new place will take some getting used to, but you will adjust to it well, I am confident of that.

Early on, you ate small plants and tiny bugs. Now you will learn to pull a delicious meal right out of the air, as you exercise your newly found long sticky tongue. You may have to acquire a taste for some of these food items, but then that is your lot in life.

Follow me now, I will show you where your special lily pad is - so when you want to sit and relax or just sun yourself, you may do so.

:) :) :):) :) :) :) :) :)

Welcome, new friend, to Clay Pond. This will be your new home if you wish it to be so!

FREDDIE THE FROG

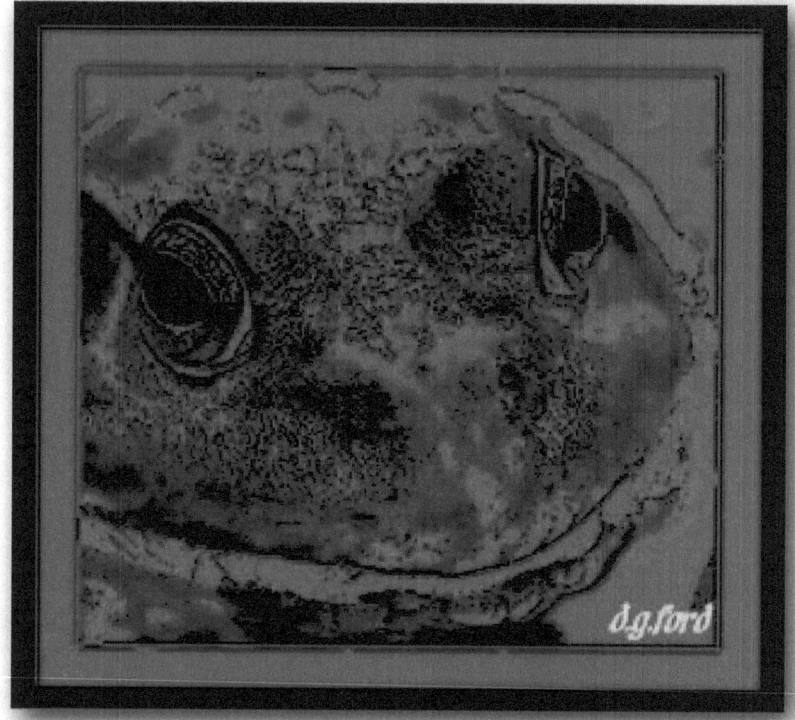

Today a couple of new friends have arrived. Freddie the Frog got tired of the same old place he had lived in forever. He knew there had to be a better place to set up his new pad. Back home he was in love with one, Olivia Frog, but she never gave him the time of day. This was reason enough to find a new pad somewhere else; maybe find love at this new location.

The other new visitor was Thaddeus Toad. This fine gentlemanly creature was well educated and brought a new look to Clay Pond. His spectacles were larger than his already huge eyes. But he was a toad; after all, and he didn't have much of a reputation among the ladies. It was always business as usual, but then every friend here was different from all others; and that was okay.

Thaddeus Toad

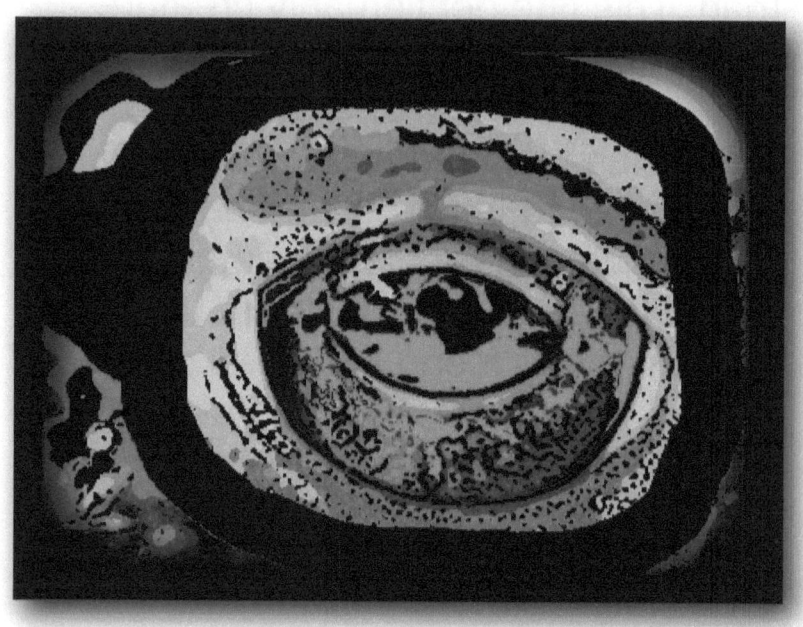

Though Thaddeus looked rather odd, compared with all of the other animals at Clay Pond, yet he was very likable. No one really understood much of what he shared, but they knew it must be something very important, since he looked and sounded like a Statesman.

He was one of the few visitors that enjoyed writing stories and sharing poetry. Even the youth came around to hear his deep tales. It was obvious that

Thaddeus was quickly becoming a favorite here on Clay Pond.

Freddie had hoped he would be welcomed here, and he was. There were some other cute frogs around the exterior of the pond, especially among the lilies. They all looked lovely surrounded by those beautiful flowers.

The problem might be that there were too many choices for Freddie. He suddenly had his eyes on a cutie. But would she really notice him? Angel was the youngest of her two sisters, Minnie and Minerva.

Her name wasn't really Angel.

It was what Freddie wanted to call her, especially with her heavenly music she made at night. He spent many evenings just outside of her pad, listening to the songs she played. One night she caught him hanging around. At first she was afraid he was stalking her; in a way he was. He hardly ever let her out of his sight.

She began seeing him around more and more. It wasn't until he stopped a predator from advancing on her that she realized he was really her protector.

A fox had also been keeping a close watch on Angel. This would be a quick morsel to grab, and he hadn't eaten in a couple of days. Angel had gotten out of the water at one point. and tried to smell the flowers on the edge of the pond.

Freddie wasn't far from her, when he spied the fox creeping up on Angel. He knew it would be a risk, but he had to save her, even if it meant sacrificing his own life to do it. The fox was in position. Freddie aimed his long sticky tongue at the fox; snapping his butt. The fox was startled, and let out a low yip. This caused Angel to leap into the pond, and swim far away from the present danger. Looking back, she saw her hero. By now, the disgruntled fox had vanished from sight.

Cindy (Angel) was her real name. She did a little investigating on her own to find out who this curious frog was who was always there, especially when she needed him. Everything she had found on him made Freddie look better and better. This was what her mom must have meant when she spoke of her finding a 'good catch'. LOL He was 'a keeper', others were saying about him.

The two began seeing more of each other, until they decided to tie the knot in their relationship. I forgot to mention that Thaddeus was a Preacher Toad, so he consented to marry them. Others would use his services also from this time forward. A female toad was watching this wedding from a distance, and was moved by Thaddeus' eloquence. The creatures at Clay Pond have their own rules about relationships. Until that knot is actually tied, living together without commitment is frowned upon.

Another beginning chapter in the life of a Clay Pond resident comes to an end, but our story isn't half over.

Now there is Thaddeus, a worthy toad, if ever there was one. He once saved his entire family from an invasion of stinging bees.

You know the type. They look at you and decide where best to plant that barbed stinger. It's best to not make eye contact with any of them, and certainly never swat at them. They don't even need a reason to sting you!

We don't need the whole hive to come after us. But Thaddeus never realized how close his family was living to a full blown bees' nest in the ground.

While his family slept he quietly removed the younger ones to another safer location. Bees sleep at night when the sun goes down, so this is the best time to escape.

Thaddeus then quietly woke up all of the older toads and slowly lead them away to where he hid the others. By the time the sun came up the next morning, all were moved to a new location far away from the bees nesting place.

All night long Thaddeus worked on this project to save his entire family from the bees. In the nick of time he was able to get the last of his relatives to safety.

Even though they were tired, groggy, and hesitant to move out of the family home, they managed to follow Thaddeus to their new living quarters.

The next day the family honored their wonderful child and relative. Most never gave Thad the time of day, but today he was their Hero.

The gal who lands this gentleman will be one lucky lady. But so far no takers, but he's a young toad and time is on his side.

If you're wondering about the young female toad that looked on him admiringly at the wedding of Freddie and Cindy, she's still around.

It might require a bolt of lightning to get him off this seat and headed in the direction of a mate, as shy as he was.

Just then, Freddie stopped by to mention to Thad that the pond was having an informal party, and all residents were asked to be in attendance. He was inquiring as to whether Thad and his young friend would be going.

Thad decided he would go in his best outfit. Could wedding bells be in his future soon, also?

SPECIAL APPEARANCE

by Basil the Frog

An Almost TRUE Fairy Tale

KEY WORDS: frog, prince, mother, nature, pond

KISS ME

Dear Mother Nature,

I must have a talk with you personally. I can not bear my life anymore in its present state. I figured you were the only one I could really go to – the only one who would understand what I am about to share. I know we haven't spoken to each other in quite a while. It's really my fault. Please read this and get back to me. I will be anxiously awaiting your response. *See my letter below.*

Dear Mother of us all,
Here is my dilemma:

You know me as Basil the Frog of Clay Pond. I was born and raised there as you know. I no longer reside there. I now live in a house. You heard me right. Let me explain.

I have been kissed by countless strange women in my time. But in an attempt to find their Prince Charming, they have gotten no where with me. The last lady to kiss me was just happy to be with me and wait for the change to take place. She even took me home with her and had a lovely aquatic room built for my pleasure.

She is a wonderful lady in waiting and I fear she will never see her dream fulfilled. I am still very much a frog, but she always makes me feel like so much more. She deserves more than I can offer her at this time.

Is there any hope I will be her Prince any time soon? Please get right back to me on this matter.

Waiting to hear,

Basil

****

So - Sir Basil,

Now I know where you went after leaving the Clay Pond. I really had no idea what had happened to you. I even questioned your friends. They stated that they had seen you with quite a few of the ladies, but that was all that they remembered.

When you leave the Nature World for the human's realm at large, I am unable to decipher your comings and goings anymore.

I do not venture into their realm. I have enough problems to sort out here without taking on the entire world.
My advice to you follows:

Dear Head in the Clouds,
   This is the real world. Tell your honey for me that kissing frogs only works in fairy tales, and to give up on you becoming anymore than what you are.

Which by the way, is a very handsome frog.
Any gal would be lucky to land a gentleman
such as you.

If only Hollywood could stop writing
'Happily Ever After' stories that spin things
all out of proportion. Look how they depict
me as a scary tyrannical female. They
believe if they cross me, I will start to throw
lightning bolts at them. How pathetic is that
– and who writes this garbage. Those
writers should have their licenses pulled.
No wonder I get so few visitors or hits on
my website.
Come back to Mother,
Mother Nature

Where to go to save the world's endangered frog and toad population.

http://www.savethefrogs.com/index.html

Click here to help save the Yellow-Legged Frogs and Yosemite Toads!

SAVE THE FROGS!

SAVE THE FROGS! is the world's leading amphibian conservation

organization. Our mission is to protect amphibian populations and to promote a society that respects and appreciates nature and wildlife. We work in California, across the USA, and around the world to prevent the extinction of amphibians, and to create a better planet for humans and wildlife.

Amphibian populations have been rapidly disappearing worldwide and nearly one-third of the world's amphibian species are on the verge of extinction. Up to 200 species have completely disappeared since 1979. Frogs and other amphibians face an array of threats from climate change to habitat destruction; pesticide use; over-collection for frog legs and dissections; invasive species; and infectious diseases spread by human activity.

Frogs eat mosquitoes; provide us with medical advances; serve as food for birds, fish and monkeys; and their tadpoles filter our drinking water. Plus frogs look and sound cool, and kids love them -- so there are lots of reasons to save the frogs!

Founded by Dr. Kerry Kriger in 2008, SAVE THE FROGS! is an IRS-approved 501(c)(3) public charity and donations are tax-deductible to the fullest extent of the law.

"When we save the frogs, we're protecting all our wildlife, all our ecosystems and all humans."
-- SAVE THE FROGS! Founder Dr. Kerry Kriger; Washington DC,
Save The Frogs Day 2011

Please visit the SAVE THE FROGS! Gift Center

You can spread the word and support our worldwide amphibian conservation efforts by ordering some eco-friendly frog merchandise from our **Gift Center**!

Please become an Official Member of SAVE THE FROGS!

The most important action any frog lover can take to help SAVE THE FROGS! is to **become an Official Member today**. Your financial support enables us to grow our movement, educate the masses, and implement on-the-ground actions that provide direct benefit to amphibians and their habitats. Just as important, the larger our supporter base, the easier it is for us to receive assistance from foundations, corporations, politicians and other nonprofits. Plus you get a great membership package when you join! So make your voice heard by joining SAVE THE FROGS! today. The frogs are disappearing fast, but we can save them -- with YOUR help. Thanks!

SAVE THE FROGS! Academy is in session

SAVE THE FROGS! Academy offers free online classes every Sunday and Wednesday. If you want to learn about frogs and how to save them, please attend! We look forward to teaching YOU how to save the frogs and make the world a better place for both humans and wildlife! Register for the next class here.

Featured Video

SAVE THE FROGS! teamed up with TED-Ed to create a video

about frog extinctions. Please watch it, share it and embed it on your website!

View more of our videos on the **SAVE THE FROGS! YouTube Channel**.

All the latest frog news is on the FrogBlog!
You can find all the frog news you could ever dream of in **The Frog Blog**! That includes website and campaign updates, new educational materials, event announcements, interviews, jobs & grants, frog stories, and amphibious news from around the world!

Please check out these pages:

HOW MUCH DO WE CARE ABOUT THESE CREATURES? SEE BELOW.

SAVE THE FROGS! Ghana

SAVE THE FROGS! COLOMBIA

SAVE THE FROGS!
Art Contest

savethefrogs.com/art

Build A Frog Pond!

savethefrogs.com/ponds

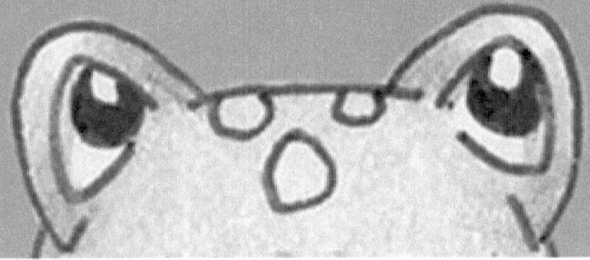

SAVE THE FROGS!
POETRY CONTEST
CASH PRIZES!

savethefrogs.com/poetry

Please donate to SAVE THE FROGS!

Your financial support makes our worldwide amphibian conservation efforts possible! SAVE THE FROGS! has many programs going on right now for which we seek funding: education and advocacy in the USA, Bangladesh, Ghana and Belize; Save The Frogs Day; frogging expeditions; getting Atrazine banned; stopping the importation of non-native bullfrogs, and more! We can only run these programs with the support of people like you. Please help out by making a tax-deductible donation today. Thanks!

Birthday Gifts for Frog Lovers

Our Spotted Treefrog Adoption Kit makes a fabulous birthday gift for any frog lover!

Spread the word

Please add our logo to your website and link to this page!

Please donate to support our efforts!

Generous supporters like you make our worldwide amphibian conservation efforts possible. Thanks for your support!

" What is there
to life if a man
cannot hear the
lonely cry of a whippoorwill
or the arguments of the frogs
around a pond at night? "

— Chief Seattle, 1854

savethefrogs.com

Other **CLAY POND** **tales by Don G. Ford from this same collection of Books; see some of them here.**

Clay Pond and Other Fish Tails by Mr. Don G. Ford

Each story stands alone. Believe it or not these are the facts and they happened to me. No matter how incredible they may seem, they are all true. Enjoy these short journeys into my life and world. You will come away remembering them, and I got to personally experience

them.
Publication Date: June 30, 2013

Clay Pond - Lady Bugley by
Mr. Don G. Ford

Clay Pond is an adventure more than just a story. You will meet new friends here that you will want to keep forever. They will become as much a part of your life once you become involved in their lives. Once you enter Clay Pond, you will find a place you can return to at different times where you can relax; a...

Publication Date: June 27, 2013

Clay Pond - What is a Woodie?
Authored by Mr. Don G. Ford, Don Ford
Edition: 1

Picture a pond full of every type of bird, fish, frog, snake and they all are going to have their own story to tell. This is Woodie's turn as he becomes the newest member of the crew. Will he be accepted or asked to leave? Every one must get along or there will be consequences.

Publication Date: Jul 08 2013

"Clay Pond - We all Love Lacy" by Mr. Don G. Ford

is now added to this series of pond stories. Many of my stories in this whole collection are based on true incidents in the writer's life.

As the reader, I hope you fall in love with this nature world as I have drawn it. The purpose of compiling these tales is to entertain, stir, or bring to remembrance some of the readers' own experiences as they step out into their own nature world around them.

You will never view a Dragonfly in the same way ever again. As a youth I was told that a Dragonfly or Darning Needle would sew up our lips if we talked too much. Not a STITCH of truth here!

Paul Smith's College grad, 1969 - Don G. Ford, called to tell us that he sold a story about Blackflies and Dragonflies to a Guidepost Magazine Imprint, Angels on Earth.

Blackflies in the Adirondack Mountains of New York? "Are you sure?" They wondered?

CLAY POND

We All Love Lacy

Don G. Ford

Other works by this same author

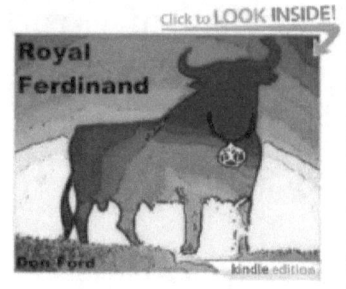

$0.99 **Nook Book**

Reading

Royal Ferdinand [NOOK

Book]Attention parents and
Grandparents. Great read!

Overview:

Friends come in all sizes, colors, and
species. Children and those young at
heart will enjoy this display of simple fun
as we look into the lives of two very
different characters, who we find in the
end are not so different. This tale is really
for the kid in all of us. A fun loving,
carefree, and learning experience for
children today.

<u>Connect the Dots</u> by Mr. Don G. Ford

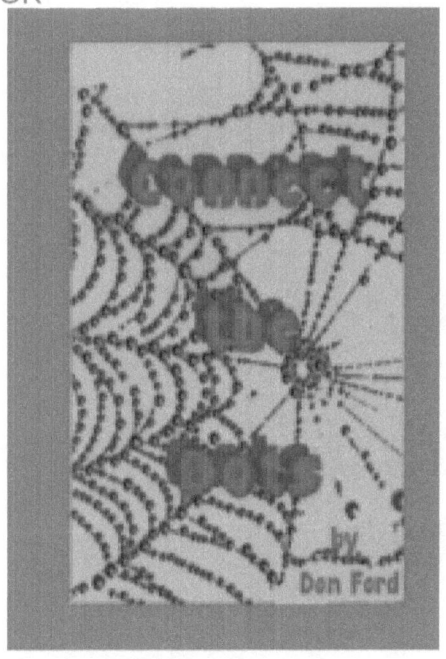

In the last seven years I have been working on short stories; a plethora of them. I have decided to compile stories for the reader along various topics. This happens to be stories that are all fiction for the most part. I hope you find this selection of tales to be entertaining and worth what you invested in...

Publication Date: February 22, 2013

Tree With the Money on it by Mr. Don G. Ford

CreateSpace Store / BOOK

Every reader should be grabbing for this book. Times are tough, and having a money tree in the back yard could spell good times for all. See for yourself. This was created with the younger reader in mind, but parents and grandparents will want to have a look. This could go nicely beside the child's bed for a...

Publication Date: June 26, 2013

Chilly The Very Warm-Blooded Polar Bear by Mr. Don G. Ford

CreateSpace Store / BOOK

Maybe the Polar Bear is what we need to watch regarding Global Warming. If they suddenly appear in our backyards, this could be a big clue that things have warmed up a whole lot and the bears are now on the move. It gives us all something to think about and its told in a fun way so that it will be a pleasure...

Publication Date: June 30, 2013

Funny Business by Mr. Don G. Ford

The purpose of this compilation of short stories, vignettes, and poems is to turn a few smiles right side up. You'll run into spiders, ghosts and even the little "Fly on the Wall". It's all in fun and for everyone's reading pleasure. If you have your boots on, jump right in. Every chapter here is a...

Publication Date: March 28, 2013

<u>Guess Who's Hiding at the Alphabet ZOO</u> by Mr. Don G. Ford

CreateSpace Store / BOOK

Life is all about variety, and no where is that truer than in the animal kingdom. There are different kinds of dogs, horses, fish, rabbits; you name it. This book will take you into the lives of many of those animals. If you didn't care before, or know that you should, remember that many of these creatures...

Publication Date: June 4, 2013

The Great Migration by Mr. Don G. Ford

CreateSpace Store / BOOK

If this story is received in the way I hope, it should be easy to see it on the large screen of the mind. It is my hope to drop the reader into the action and make them feel like they are there experiencing it each step of the way. I hope you will care about each character and their role in this adventure as...

Publication Date: April 1, 2013

Floyd the Dog Story Book
Commemorative by Mr. Don G. Ford
CreateSpace Store / BOOK

Here is the new Book that I would love you to have a look at. The cover says it all. Michael St. John, Publisher of "Floyd the Dog", a Portuguese Book Club, has accepted so many of my stories that it only makes sense to honor him in this way. There's something in these tales for everyone. You can take this...
Publication Date: June 20, 2013

All books are listed here in a link.
http://tinyurl.com/l4al233
CONTACT AUTHOR ABOUT SIGNING